30

AFRICAN AMERICANS
in the Vietnam War

DIANE CANWELL and JON SUTHERLAND

WORLD ALMANAC® LIBRARY

Please visit our web site at: www.worldalmanaclibrary.com
For a free color catalog describing World Almanac® Library's list of high-quality books
and multimedia programs, call 1-800-848-2928 (USA) or 1-800-387-3178 (Canada).
World Almanac® Library's fax: (414) 332-3567.

Library of Congress Cataloging-in-Publication Data

Sutherland, Jonathan.
    African Americans in the Vietnam War / by Jon Sutherland and Diane Canwell.
        p. cm. — (The American experience in Vietnam)
    Includes bibliographical references and index.
    ISBN 0-8368-5772-0 (lib. bdg.)
    ISBN 0-8368-5779-8 (softcover)
    1. Vietnamese Conflict, 1961-1975—African Americans—Juvenile literature.
    2. Racism—United States—Juvenile literature. I. Canwell, Diane. II. Title.
    III. Series.
    DS559.8.B55S87   2005
    959.704'34'08996073—dc22   2004058096

First published in 2005 by
World Almanac® Library
330 West Olive Street, Suite 100
Milwaukee, WI 53212 USA

Developed by Amber Books Ltd.
Editor: James Bennett
Designer: Colin Hawes
Photo research: Natasha Jones
World Almanac® Library editors: Mark Sachner and Alan Wachtel
World Almanac® Library art direction: Tammy West
World Almanac® Library production: Jessica Morris

Picture Acknowledgements
Camera Press: 4; Cody Images (www.codyimages.com): cover (top left), 16, 22, 29;
Corbis: cover (main), 6, 9, 10, 11, 12, 14, 18, 19, 23, 24, 26, 31, 33, 36, 37, 40, 43;
Getty Images: 27, 28, 34, 41, 42; U.S. D.O.D.: 8; U.S. National Archives: 1, 4 (top left),
21, 39.

Printed in Canada

1 2 3 4 5 6 7 8 9 09 08 07 06 05

About the Authors

JON SUTHERLAND and **DIANE CANWELL** have worked as a writing
team since 1990, writing for books and magazines on a wide range of historical
and military subjects. Jon Sutherland's publications include the 900-page
African Americans at War: An Encyclopedia, while Diane Canwell has authored
books on various aspects of military history. They live in Norfolk, U.K.

Table of Contents

Words that appear in the glossary are printed in **boldface** type the first time they occur in the text

Introduction

The Vietnam War (1954–1975) was part of a larger conflict known as the Second Indochina War, which raged in Southeast Asia and involved the nations of Cambodia, Laos, and Vietnam. From 1946 until 1954, the Vietnamese had fought for independence from France during the First Indochina War. When the French were defeated, the country was divided into North and South Vietnam. Vietnamese communists controlled North Vietnam and wanted to unify Vietnam under communist rule. Non-communist Vietnamese controlled the South. In the 1950s, the United States and the Soviet Union were in the early years of their struggle over political, economic, and military influence in various parts of the world. Known as the Cold War, this struggle did not pit each nation against the other directly. Rather, each supported other countries that were squared off against one another. In the 1950s, the United States began training South Vietnam's army, while the Soviet Union and China backed communist North Vietnam. By the mid-1960s, U.S. forces fought alongside the Army of the Republic of Vietnam (ARVN) against the North Vietnamese Army (NVA) and the National Front for the Liberation of Vietnam (NLF).

Back in 1948, President Harry S. Truman had issued an executive order that aimed to bring an end to official racial **segregation** within the ranks of the U.S. military forces. This was significant for all minorities, but especially for African Americans, who had a long history of fighting in every single conflict the United States had been involved in and for whom the civil rights issue was beginning to heat up. Although the process of military desegregation had begun during the Korean War (1950–1953), the Vietnam War was the first conflict in which an entirely desegregated military fought. In the early years of the war, African American soldiers in Vietnam took the brunt of the casualties, as they were often assigned to the front lines. Following severe criticism, the armed services redressed the issue, and overall, African American losses were seen to be in proportion to those suffered by other ethnic groups fighting in the U.S. forces.

For African Americans, the Vietnam War was a war in which they not only had to cope with enemy fire, but also had to tolerate racism and violence within their own ranks. The tensions and protests that swept the United States in the 1960s were also felt in Vietnam. Race riots and civil rights demonstrations occurred in military camps just as they occurred in cities back home. African Americans and other minority groups tended to keep to themselves while at base camp, and certain bars and rest areas were unofficially off-limits to people of different races.

Combat, however, had a unifying effect, and in the throes of a battle, it was a person's valor and courage that mattered and not the color of his skin. Ultimately, soldiers returning home after the Vietnam War found themselves welcomed by bitterness and scorn, regardless of skin color, by those who had not supported the United States' involvement in Vietnam.

Below: This map shows North and South Vietnam and the surrounding area. Key regions, cities, and military bases are indicated.

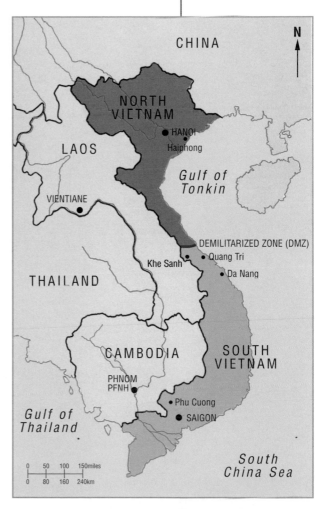

5

The Background

Right: A machine-gunner takes a break at the Tan An Delta in 1968. This year saw African Americans contributing up to 20 percent of combat troops and around 14 percent of U.S. fatalities.

"In the average rifle company, the strength was fifty percent composed of Negroes, Southwestern Mexicans, Puerto Ricans, Guamanians, Nisei, and so on. But a real, cross-section of American youth? Almost never."

—General S. L. A. Marshall recalling the Vietnam-era U.S. Army, quoted in Myra MacPherson's *Long Time Passing*, 1984

African Americans, like other minorities, have served in various roles in the United States' wars and conflicts since the United States was born. The inclusion of other races among white soldiers, however, was often a matter of simply needing the manpower as opposed to a desire to ensure equality. As a result, segregation, racism, and conflict was often a part of daily life for these soldiers, and African Americans at times found themselves fighting two wars: the war the United States was involved in and the war against **discrimination**.

SEGREGATION IN THE ARMED FORCES

African Americans have been a sizable minority in the U.S. for several generations. They have fought in all of the nation's wars and internal conflicts since the colonial period. Upwards of 200,000 African Americans fought for the Union during the Civil War (1861–1865), and regulars and volunteers were committed to Cuba in the war against Spain in the 1890s. Two whole African American **infantry** divisions were engaged in Europe during World War I (1914–1918). Segregated divisions manned naval vessels, air force fighters, and tank destroyers, and fought as infantry and U.S. Marines, during World War II (1939–1945). Yet along with their duties, they had to cope with segregation and **marginalization**. White officers commanded African Americans in uniform, and white officials in the armed forces and in Washington, D.C., determined their roles and fates.

Right: Men of the Ninety-third Division fight in the trenches during World War I. Collectively, African Americans suffered 750 deaths and 5,000 wounded during the war.

During World War I, Brigadier General Harvey Jerrey stated, "It is not the policy of the United States Army to encourage or permit the formation of distinctive brigades, regiments, battalions, or other organizations composed exclusively or primarily of members of any race, creed, political, or social group." However, this was just an official statement; in reality, segregation was alive and well in the U.S. armed forces until well after the end of World War II.

DESEGREGATION IN THE MILITARY

In 1948, President Harry S. Truman ordered the U.S. military establishment to desegregate. The process of desegregation, however, was still ongoing during the Korean War (1950–1953). According to the Truman Presidential Museum and Library, the order declared that "there shall be equality of treatment and opportunity for all persons in the armed services without regard

CAMP LEJEUNE

In the evening of July 20, 1969, a serious racial disturbance occurred at Marine Corps Base Camp Lejeune, North Carolina. After a party, a group of white marines on their way back to the base were assaulted by an estimated thirty to fifty African American marines. Fifteen white marines were injured. One victim, Corporal Edward E. Bankston, a thrice-wounded veteran of Vietnam, died seven days later of massive head injuries. Others were stabbed and beaten.

A subcommittee convened to handle the investigation came to the conclusion that the racial disturbances on the base were caused by militant African Americans who had fanned the flames of suspicion and misconceptions between white and black marines, and accepted that greater education and more mature leadership were required to prevent further incidents of this type.

Left: African American recruits at Camp Lejeune, North Carolina, march in parade drill practice in March 1943. The black marines became known as the Montford Point Marines, as they were assigned to this segregated training camp.

to race, color, religion or national origin." Truman also established a presidential committee to oversee the desegregation of military units. Truman's order, however, met strong resistance from elements within the military establishment, which was slow to act according to his order. By the beginning of the Korean War, most military units remained segregated. Under continued pressure from the administration, however, the process of desegregation was accelerated. Ninety percent of United States military units were integrated by the end of the Korean War in 1953. The Vietnam War, therefore, marked the first major combat deployment of desegregated U.S. military forces.

Right: Radio operator Clarence Whitmore of the Twenty-fourth Infantry in Korea takes a break near Sangju on August 9, 1950.

PROTESTERS AND THE MILITARY

The Civil Rights movement was closely allied with the antiwar movement, with protestors on both sides claiming that the war in Vietnam was taking money and attention away from the problems of African Americans at home. By the late 1960s, civil rights and antiwar demonstrations were clearly beginning to have an impact on the feelings of troops stationed in and around Vietnam. African American naval airman Bill Norman returned for a third tour in Vietnam in 1969, by which time things had clearly changed. Military personnel were now questioning the war, not just the protestors at home.

As Norman recalled: "I began questioning the rationale for what we were doing and the effectiveness of our efforts. It was no longer a war in which a few people were being killed. Large, large numbers of people were being killed. And everybody knew about it. It was in the papers, on the television. And there were demonstrations against the war back home."

Left: An antiwar "Guerrilla Theater" takes place on Capitol Hill in the early 1970s. Many of the protestors were Vietnam veterans. Antiwar rallies in 1970 led to six deaths and the closure of four hundred university campuses.

MINORITIES IN THE ARMED FORCES

Although the policy of desegregation within the U.S. armed forces began in the 1950s, Vietnam was the first conflict in which truly multicultural platoons fought. Prior to the Korean War, which had seen the end of official segregation, ethnic minorities had experienced a long involvement in the U.S. military. African Americans had served in mainly segregated units since the eighteenth century, and in all of the conflicts affecting the United States, both internally and internationally.

Native Americans were highly prized scouts and interpreters during the long series of wars along the Western frontier. A remarkable forty-two thousand Native Americans served in Vietnam, 90 percent of whom were volunteers.

Although Japanese Americans were initially **interned** when the U.S. entered the war in 1941, two Japanese American units were formed in 1943 and served in Italy. Asian Americans proved invaluable in Vietnam, where their broad understanding of the customs and cultures of the region, as well as their linguistic skills, made them useful liaison staff.

With a long tradition of service dating back to at least the Civil War, Hispanic Americans also added to the U.S. military vision of a multicultural platoon. Some eighty-thousand Hispanic Americans served in Vietnam, thirteen of whom were awarded the Medal of Honor. Like African Americans in the early days of the war, they too would suffer a disproportionate number of casualties, a full 19 percent of the total, despite the fact that they only accounted for 4.5 percent of the U.S. population.

Left: A racially mixed group of U.S. Marines approach the beach in an amphibious assault in the Rung Sat Special Zone, a warren of inland waterways vital for access to the port of Saigon.

A BLACK MAN'S FIGHT?

As U.S. involvement in Vietnam grew, some protestors claimed that African Americans accounted for a disproportionate share of those drafted. It was also claimed that African Americans faced a much higher probability of being assigned to the front line. The draft itself was a major cause of concern. College students and those doing a variety of essential civilian jobs—usually white, middle class young men—could defer the draft. The early draftees tended to be the poorer, less educated urban classes of which African Americans formed a major percentage.

In the early years of the Vietnam War, African Americans accounted for a disproportionately high number of combat troops committed to Vietnam. In the period 1961–1966, African Americans accounted for around 10 percent of U.S. forces, from a population of 13 percent of the nation's people. However, in 1965 alone, one African American soldier was killed for every four white soldiers. In 1968, a year for which we have accurate figures, we see the reason for this imbalance. By then, African Americans provided 12 percent of the army and marine contingents, but upwards of 50

Right: A U.S. Marine patrols in the Demilitarized Zone (DMZ), near Quang Tri in 1968.

percent of the front-line troops, especially the rifle squads and fire teams, were black. In that year, U.S. forces numbered 536,000. African Americans accounted for 9.8 percent of this number, yet they composed nearly 20 percent of all combat troops, and 14.1 percent of the 14,592 killed that year were African American.

In 1966, President Lyndon Johnson launched Project 100,000, aimed at increasing recruitment into the U.S. military by reducing the entrance requirements. Of the 350,000 men recruited under the program, 41 percent were African American, and of these, 40 percent drew combat assignments.

Statistics such as these prompted Dr. Martin Luther King, Jr., and other leaders of the Civil Rights movement, to claim that the Vietnam War was "a white man's war, a black man's fight." Under extreme pressure from the Civil Rights movement and the White House, adjustments were made to the deployment of African American soldiers, and by the end of the conflict, African Americans had suffered 12.1 percent of the total casualties, a number that was closer to their civilian population ratio of 12.5 percent.

About 275,000 African American men and women served in Vietnam, making up 10.6 percent of the total committed forces. A high percentage of volunteers were African American, especially toward the close of the war. In 1964, African Americans accounted for 9 percent of the army forces; by 1976, they provided 15 percent. African American officers had doubled in number over the same period but still accounted for only 4 percent of all officers.

RECRUITMENT AND BOOT CAMP

For all those facing boot camp, basic training in the U.S. military service came as a distinct shock—particularly for African Americans. It was a long-standing U.S. Army tradition for drill sergeants to be white men, recruited from the Deep South. Many of these men had begun their military service when the army was segregated, and this was reflected in their attitude toward African Americans. In turn, African American recruits resented taking orders from white southerners, sensing uncomfortable echoes of the slavery era.

Sometimes the recruitment system would clearly favor white recruits. Wayne Smith, an African American from Providence, Rhode Island, joined the U.S. Army in November 1968. He had signed up on the "buddy system," which promised that friends would serve together. His friend, however, a white recruit, was assigned an office post in the United States.

On Patrol

Right: Two men of the twenty-fifth Infantry Division carry a wounded comrade to an evacuation point during Operation Baker in the Duc Pho region of Vietnam.

The Vietnam War may have been the first major combat deployment of desegregated U.S. troops, but it didn't always feel desegregated to the soldiers fighting the war, nor to the U.S. citizens observing it. In the early years of the war, the statistics show that African Americans especially were being singled out for combat assignments and that more officers were white than black and received less risky assignments.

THE EXPERIENCE

Even as late as 1970, as African American career officer William De Shields discovered, the majority of front-line troops were black. De Shields was assigned to Vietnam in 1970 to command the Twenty-seventh Composite Maintenance Battalion based in Quang Tri, to the south of the North Vietnamese border. Aside from the twelve hundred men under his direct command, he also had responsibility for several other, smaller units, dealing with ammunition, transportation, and fuel. Of his command, De Shields said: "I noted many of the front line soldiers tended to be blacks, Hispanics, Italians, and low-income whites. During the initial phases of the Vietnam War, casualties among blacks far exceeded their number in the population."

Captain George Forrest of the Fifth Cavalry, who fought at the Battle of the Ia Drang Valley in November 1965, received wise advice from his father back in 1961 when he joined the basic officer training course at Fort Benning, Georgia: "Black men have to be twice as good, twice as smart, and three times as lucky." Forrest's first tour in Vietnam saw him in action with the Eleventh Air Assault Division. He was one of several African American combat company commanders; 25 percent of his company was either African American or Hispanic. An African American officer told reporter Thomas Johnson in 1968: "They [African American teenage soldiers] feel they're the first Negroes to fight because their history books told only of white soldiers, and their movies showed that John Wayne and Errol Flynn won all American wars."

Dr. Martin Luther King, Jr., summed up the resentment felt by many of those campaigning for equal rights in the United States when he said: "We have been repeatedly faced with the cruel wrong of watching Negro and white boys on TV screens as they kill and die together for a nation that has been unable to seat them in the same schools. So we watch them in brutal **solidarity** burning the huts of a poor village, but we realize that they would never live on the same block in Detroit."

Below: Battalion commander Lieutenant Colonel Edward Meyer comforts a wounded trooper after an engagement with the Viet Cong in the mountainous area around Bong Son.

HELMET AND FLAK JACKET GRAFFITI

In Vietnam, drawing graffiti art with permanent marker pens was commonplace. Soldiers inscribed poems, word slang, names, pictures of their girlfriends, drawings, and anything else they liked on their helmet covers and **flak jackets**. Some graffiti had meaning only to its wearer. Others used graffiti to make a statement about the war. Lieutenant Colonel Steve Richmond (USMC) recalled a piece of antiwar graffiti worn by one of the members of his troop:

"He wasn't a model Marine—certainly by today's standards. He wore braided bracelets and necklaces of peace beads, and his graffiti-decorated helmet proclaimed his involvement with the Black Power activism prevalent at the time. I had seen him on more than one occasion at informal discipline hearings…. As much as he complained, [however,] he went back out when the time came. The night the North Vietnamese hit us, he was there. When an RPG [rocket-propelled grenade] hit his hole, he did not cave. When his partner took a round and went down, he stood over him in the hole and fought it out. It wasn't a glorious death, but he died a Marine, holding his position, facing the enemy, rifle in hand. And I don't much care what he had written on his helmet."

Above: A U.S. Marine takes a break during fighting in Hue in early 1968. His helmet cover—reading "born by accident"—expresses the resignation felt by many young men drafted to fight in Vietnam.

19

AFRICAN AMERICAN OFFICERS

One factor leading to accusations of racism in the military was that in the early years of the war very few African Americans served in command positions. This in turn caused low morale among African Americans in the enlisted ranks and often led to disciplinary problems. Maurice Morton saw the potential impact of having few minority officers when he served as an Army pilot in Vietnam. Of the 120 men in each of the two companies in which he served, only one officer was black. "It caused some resentment among the enlisted men," said Morton. "It does cause some problems when you look around and there are no black officers."

In response to these inequalities, the armed services moved to increase and train the number of minority officers. Although the percentage of African American officers doubled between 1964 and 1976, they still accounted for less than 4 percent of the total number of officers. In 1968, black enrollment at West Point and Annapolis was less than 1 percent, and by 1975, barely 3 percent of commissioned officers were African American.

LIFE ON PATROL

In spite of the widely-held belief that African Americans suffered a higher number of casualties than white soldiers, there were still plenty of instances of solidarity and **camaraderie** among troops during the Vietnam War.

In the initial years of the Vietnam War, a tradition existed of declaring a **truce** for a few days during Tet, the Vietnamese New

Left: U.S. Marines await pickup by a C-123 airplane on February 22, 1969. Air mobility was vital for United States forces during the Vietnam War.

Below: An African American soldier carries the heavy M60 machine gun.

Year, to allow Vietnamese people on both sides to celebrate this holiday. In January 1968, however, which was when Tet fell that year, the communists announced a truce but then launched an attack on almost every major city and province in South Vietnam. The attack, which saw U.S. troops come under heavy fire, was known as the Tet Offensive. During the Tet Offensive, Sergeant Major Edgar Huff, a veteran African American who had served in the marines during World War II, was awarded the Bronze Star for saving one of his men, a radio operator who was white. While Huff ran across an open field toward the radio operator (named Rick), a bullet hit his head, but his helmet saved him. When Huff reached the trench in which Rick was pinned, a fragmentation grenade wounded Huff in the shoulder and arm.

Then, as Huff recalled, "…our people opened up all they had. And the [Viet] Cong started moving back. And the colonel came out to help me with the stretcher to bring Rick back…. And Rick wrote me this letter. It says 'Sergeant Major, I thank you for my life.' Hell, he was one of my men. Black or white, I would have done the same even if I got shot to hell in the process…. I knew I might get killed, saving a white boy. But he was my man. That's what happened."

CARRYING THE PIG

The U.S. 0.3-inch (7.62–mm) M60 machine gun was the most prevalent weapon of its type used during the Vietnam War. Veterans have recalled that African Americans were often assigned to carry the heavy M60. It was nicknamed "the pig" for the grunting sound it made when fired.

COLOR NOT AN ISSUE

African American Daniel "Chappie" James, a World War II fighter-bomber veteran, flew seventy-eight combat missions in Vietnam. Flying an F-4 Phantom II as wing vice commander of the Eighth Fighter Tactical Wing, he was hit by antiaircraft fire on a mission over Hanoi. The aircraft was crippled, so James radioed for an airborne tanker and ordered the rest of his flight, which was dangerously low on fuel, to rendezvous for refueling without him. The pilots in his flight—who were predominantly white—refused to leave him and pretended that their radios were defective. The whole flight managed to rendezvous with the tanker and got home safely. James was delighted, but not surprised, at the actions of his crew. "We don't hate each other after all," he said. "It's really not necessary and we can't afford it."

James later addressed a group of Air Force Association officers, summing up the patriotism, determination, and resolve illustrated by so many African Americans during the Vietnam War. He said, "I'm a citizen of the United States of America and I'm no second-class citizen either and no man here is, unless he thinks like one and reasons like one and performs like one."

THE UNIFYING EFFECT OF COMBAT

After future Secretary of State Colin Powell's first tour of Vietnam in the early 1960s, he returned to the United States.

Above: General "Chappie" James, a major during the Korean War, was one of the few African American combat jet pilots in Vietnam.

Right: An African American U.S. Marine listens to his radio equipment during a lull in shelling during the siege of Khe Sanh in March 1968.

On television, he saw a friend he'd grown up with in New York, Major Antonio "Tony" Mavroudis, promoting integration. Mavroudis said: "Race did not matter out here; it doesn't exist. We are all soldiers. The only color we know is khaki and green. The color of the mud and the color of the blood are all the same."

The experience described by Major Mavroudis (who was killed during his second tour of duty in Vietnam) reflected the experience of many front-line soldiers. Milton Lee Olive III joined the army in Chicago in 1964 and began his tour of duty in Vietnam in June 1965. In the early morning of October 22, 1965, Olive and his company were landed by helicopter in enemy-held countryside in the area around Phu Cuong. As his citation later read, Olive's unit was ambushed and "subjected to a heavy volume of enemy gunfire and pinned down temporarily. It retaliated by assaulting the Viet Cong positions, causing the enemy to flee."

After this initial engagement, Olive and four other paratroopers were moving through the jungle when a Viet Cong soldier threw a hand grenade into their midst. Walking beside Olive were two other African American paratroopers, who took cover as the enemy sprang the ambush. With bullets thudding into the tree stumps around them and grenades being thrown in their direction, the paratroopers began to return fire. Suddenly, another grenade landed a foot from the unit's leader (who was white), and without a second thought, Olive grabbed the explosive and pushed it under his body, absorbing the explosion and killing himself. About twelve paratroopers were wounded, but there were no other fatalities. Olive's family was awarded the Medal of Honor on his behalf on April 21, 1966, by President Lyndon B. Johnson at the White House. If Olive's tragic tale tells us anything, we see in combat that race and ethnic background were unimportant and that mutual respect, regardless of color, led many to make sacrifices for their fellow men.

Day-to-Day Life

Right: A mixed group of U.S. Marines take a quick break at Khe Sanh in 1968. Khe Sanh was a strategic U.S. Marine base.

Although racial **stereotypes**, discrimination, and segregation clearly had their roots in U.S. society at large, they also manifested themselves in ways that were often subtle but no less damaging. For example, a large map of the United States was painted on the bulkheads of the passenger lounges of the ships taking the soldiers to war in Vietnam. Each state had a picture depicting what the state had to offer. Texas had cowboys and longhorn cattle, and Florida had waterskiers, but Georgia showed a black man eating watermelon, and other Southern states illustrated African Americans working in the cotton fields. The films en route, which dated from World War II, were no better. One starred Willie Best playing a lazy, superstitious black man. Another showed actor Manton Moreland stealing chickens. Despite the camaraderie and cohesion that often developed between men in a platoon or company, segregation was still a way of life, even if it was voluntary in some cases.

SEGREGATION AS A PART OF DAILY LIFE

Vietnam was a confusing mix of segregation and solidarity. Colin Powell was a young captain in the 1960s. He went on to head the armed services during the Gulf War (1990–1991) and was made Secretary of State in 2001. When recalling the reality of combat missions and the situation back at camp, Powell stated, "Our men in the field, trudging through elephant grass under hostile fire, did not have time to be hostile toward each other. But bases like Duc Pho were increasingly divided by the same racial polarization that had begun to plague Americans during the sixties. The base contained dozens of new men waiting to be sent out to the field and short-timers wanting to go home. For both groups, the unifying force of a shared mission and shared danger did not exist."

Harold Hayward, an African American West Point graduate of 1944, began his Vietnam tour as a staff officer at U.S. Army

Above: President Lyndon B. Johnson meets troops of the 101st Airborne Division at Fort Campbell, Kentucky, in July 1966.

Headquarters in Saigon and was later transferred to the 101st Airborne Division. He recalled the three- to five-day "stand-down" periods between missions: "Befitting their positions, the NCOs [non-commissioned officers] would collectively set themselves apart during a stand down. But I was somewhat surprised to observe the line-soldiers self-segregated immediately. Blacks staked out their territory in one part of the rest area while whites occupied another. Perhaps I was in error, but I sensed that the segregation was instigated primarily by the black troops and that the white soldiers were on the whole, indifferent to the arrangement."

Not all whites were indifferent, however. Merrill Dorsey of Maryland joined the marines in 1968; early in 1969, just after the birth of his daughter, he was sent to Vietnam. For some time, Dorsey never received any mail from his wife or family. It then became clear that a white marine from Alabama was hiding it. Dorsey recalled: "I confronted him, and he pushed me back. I'm only 125 pounds (57 kilograms), so you can push me back, but I can hold my own." The white marine knocked Dorsey down several times, but he kept getting up again. When the white marine finally told him to stay down, Dorsey said, "I got a couple of good licks in, but that was all I got. He knocked me down again. Afterwards, I got my mail from him, and he and I became friends."

THE OFFICIAL VIEW OF SEGREGATION

In 1967, the Department of Defense sent an investigative group to Vietnam led by African American L. Howard Bennett. The group was tasked with investigating racism and segregation among the

Below: U.S. Marines defend their camp with metal drum and sandbag emplacements at Khe Sanh in early 1968.

Right: White U.S. soldiers and South Vietnamese relax in Annie's Bar near Da Nang in March 1968. The white soldiers would not have been welcome in other bars in the same town, frequented only by African Americans.

AFTER-HOURS SEGREGATION

African American Joe Anderson entered West Point in 1961, just one of six blacks in a class of 950. He graduated in 1965 and was sent to Vietnam in 1966, three weeks after he got married. He remembered the brief respite of leave from the field: "Usually when we had R and R [Rest and Recreation], I left the country and was not in the rear echelons where there was racial trouble. When there were arguments, it wasn't about sex; the prostitution system was not segregated. But race came into play over music; the troops fought over soul versus country and western."

This situation reflects what Medal of Honor winner Louis Rocco, who served two tours in Vietnam, saw among the different groups there segregating themselves after hours: "The only time that I actually saw the separation was in the bars. And the thing was that nobody segregated the bars but the people themselves...They went where they felt comfortable, where they could enjoy a good time."

Left: A U.S. sailor replenishes the shells in a gun turret on a vessel in the Gulf of Tonkin. Compared to those serving on land, his was a relatively easy life, and his chances of completing his tour of duty without being wounded or killed were much higher.

troops. Bennett concluded that although the men ignored skin color under fire, there were strong racial tensions and potentially violent situations in the rear echelons (the support troops who did not actually engage the enemy). He concluded that the "agitated, hostile, and in conflict" men, both black and white, posed enormous dangers to the United States when they came home after their tours. Unfortunately, the investigating committee's findings were largely ignored.

Jesse Brewer III, who was assigned to the Ninth Marines at Khe Sanh in 1968, concurred with Bennett's findings. In an interview, Brewer said, "Most of the racial problems occurred in the rear. When Martin Luther King, Jr., was killed, things back there were really tense. At times, it was more dangerous in the rear areas than out on patrol. There were no programs of which I was aware, designed to develop good relationships between people of different races."

STAKING OUT TERRITORY

Regardless of whether there were official programs or not, many did what they could to limit segregation and racism, knowing there were more important things to worry about. Fred Black, the son of an African American officer who had served in the Twenty-fourth Infantry, reported to Vietnam in July 1969. Of his experience, Black said: "We had very few racial problems in the combat units, and those occurred when we stood down in the rear. In the field, people depended on each other because they wanted to go home in one piece. In the rear, they drank and became less guarded about revealing their feelings about different races. This cut both ways. Three black guys told a white guy in their squad he could not sleep in their bunker because they declared it 'black only' territory. We got on that real fast, and the ringleader was disciplined."

Left: At an antiwar rally in Washington, D.C., in 1967, a female protestor holds a placard that illustrates the divide between many African Americans' experiences at home and the role they were expected to play in Vietnam. The wording is derived from a statement attributed to the boxer Muhammad Ali.

According to the report published by the U.S. Army Center of Military History entitled "Military and the Media 1968–1973," the Inspector General of Military Assistance Command, Vietnam (MACV) received 2,628 race complaints. Some 146 were substantiated. Of the rest of the complaints, the report stated: "The remaining cases are partially substantiated, in that there is evidence that race is a factor, but discrimination or prejudice were not causes."

RACE RELATIONS WITH THE VIETNAMESE

When it came to relations between African Americans and the Vietnamese, the North Vietnamese, aware of racial problems in the United States, could not understand why African Americans were fighting what they saw as a white imperialist war. It is believed that North Vietnamese political officers targeted African Americans in the hope that they would desert and speak out against America's involvement in Vietnam. The South Vietnamese didn't seem to discriminate against any minorities—the prostitutes, drug dealers, and others who took the soldiers' money certainly didn't.

According to Jan Scruggs, a decorated infantry veteran who led the effort to establish a national memorial to Vietnam veterans in Washington, D.C., many Americans of all races tended to dehumanize the Vietnamese. In a television interview, Scruggs said, "One of the interesting things that I found about the Vietnam experience was that it gave individuals an opportunity to experience racism themselves. It was a chance really for black soldiers, Hispanic soldiers, and Caucasian soldiers to become racists because everyone began using the term 'gook' [derogatory term for the Vietnamese]. And everyone hated the 'gooks' and 'didn't we kill a lot of gooks the other night,' and that type of thing. So, everyone got to see and feel really the ugliest side of racial and ethnic hatred."

NO ANSWER TO THE CALL

Left: A Marine takes a short nap during the battle of Hue, February 23, 1968. He rests still draped in his machine gun belts, with his machine gun close at hand.

Many African American soldiers on the front line in Vietnam could never, and have never to this day, been able to answer a frequent Viet Cong call heard in the middle of the night, "Why are you fighting us, black soldiers?" It seemed to many that the Viet Cong knew that African Americans who suffered from inequalities in the United States were willingly supporting a white-dominated military.

Civil Rights

Right: This protestor was demonstrating on August 17, 1966, at a Senate investigation into civil rights groups involved in antiwar activities.

While the Civil Rights movement did make its presence felt among the soldiers in Vietnam, the reality was that from the outset troops assigned to Vietnam were apart, both socially and geographically, from the United States. When they returned, it was to a changed nation.

THE CIVIL RIGHTS MOVEMENT

The Civil Rights movement was a political, legal, and social struggle to gain full citizenship rights for African Americans and to achieve racial equality. The primary focus of the Civil Rights movement was to challenge segregation. Individuals and civil rights organizations fought discrimination with a variety of activities, including protest marches, **boycotts**, and a refusal to abide by segregation laws.

Benjamin Oliver Davis, Jr., was the first African American to graduate from West Point in the twentieth century. In World War II he commanded the first African American air force unit (the Tuskegee Airmen) and went on to become the first black four-star general in the air force. Davis recalled: "We [he and his wife Agnes] left the United States in 1965 before the height of the violence by white reactionaries, and returned in the summer of 1968, when some of the major actions by black activists had already taken place. When news of the happenings in the States did reach us abroad during those years, often on Armed Forces Radio, it was sketchy and out of date."

By the late 1960s, civil rights activists such as Martin Luther King, Jr., had become increasingly critical of the Vietnam War. On August 23, 1966, boxer Muhammad Ali applied to the Selective Service for status as a **conscientious objector** on religious grounds. He was quoted as saying: "I ain't got no quarrel with the Viet Cong.... No Viet Cong ever called me nigger." Ali also said: "No, I am not going 10,000 miles to help

Above: Pictured in March 1966, boxer Muhammad Ali points to a newspaper headline showing that many others share his views about the Vietnam War. He would later refuse to be **inducted** into the army.

murder, kill, and burn other people to simply help continue the domination of white slave masters over dark people the world over. This is the day and age when such evil injustice must come to an end." Ali became embroiled in a vicious political and legal battle that ultimately culminated in his being stripped of his boxing title and branded as a draft dodger. In 1971, almost five years into Ali's legal battle, the United States Supreme Court overturned his draft conviction.

RETURNING HOME

As the Vietnam War began to wind down, it became obvious that returning soldiers, with their memories of the horrors of combat, would have to face an uncertain future in a changed United States. African American Wayne Smith recalled how he felt after thirty-days' leave back in the United States during his

THE BLACK POWER MOVEMENT

Left: Floyd B. McKissick walks on a picket line outside the Apollo Theatre in Harlem, in New York City, on July 22, 1966. McKissick was the director of the Congress of Racial Equality (CORE). He supported calls to cease the drafting of African Americans to fight in Vietnam.

The Black Power movement consisted of African Americans uniting in actively resisting discrimination, often calling for an independent course of action from movements that included whites. Black Power emphasized self-defense tactics, self-determination, political and economic power, and racial pride. Black Power represented both a conclusion to the Civil Rights movement and a reaction against the racism that persisted despite the efforts of African American activists during the early 1960s. The meaning of Black Power was debated vigorously while the movement was in progress. To some, it represented African Americans' insistence on racial dignity and self-reliance, which was usually interpreted as economic and political independence, as well as freedom from white authority.

Above: African American veteran Frank Goins holds his Silver Star, Bronze Star, and Purple Heart, received for bravery in Vietnam. Goins served in the U.S. First Infantry Division during the conflict. Some twenty African Americans won the Medal of Honor during the Vietnam conflict.

tour of duty in 1969: "It was one of the worst mistakes I ever made. I came home and it was stranger than going to Vietnam. My value system changed. Much of what I believed in was a lie. I had no understanding of the future at all. I couldn't wait to get back to Vietnam." Three weeks after he returned from Vietnam, at the age of twenty, Smith was convicted of manslaughter and sentenced to ten years in prison. He is now executive director of the Justice Project in Washington, D.C.

African American David Parks was sent to Vietnam as a radio operator. On January 31, 1967, he wrote in his diary: "Sgt. Paulson hand-picks the men for this job [patrols]. So far he's fingered only Negroes and Puerto Ricans. I think he is trying to tell us something." Parks was later wounded by shrapnel from a mine, and when he returned to the United States, he followed in his father's footsteps as a photographer. He began photographing the antiwar protests in New York and Washington, D.C. Parks found that he was "shaken by the hate slogans that were shouted at the soldiers and police. I strongly felt that the men still fighting in Vietnam deserved our full support." Men who had recently returned from Vietnam often faced these protestors. Parks witnessed this and recalled: "The soldiers didn't retaliate because they were tired, sick, and broken. I couldn't take pictures. It was impossible to do anything. I hated what I had seen and I hated America for it."

Many of those who returned found that they had more in common with one another than with the rest of the United States. The war had changed them, and, above all, the war had

MARTIN LUTHER KING, JR.

Dr. Martin Luther King, Jr., leader of the Civil Rights movement and a prominent African American leader, voiced his disapproval of the threatening, anti-white message often associated with Black Power. Encouraging African Americans to be proud of their race and to appreciate their heritage, King also advised them to "avoid the error of building a distrust for all white people."

Left: An anti-Vietnam War demonstration takes place in New York on March 16, 1967. Martin Luther King, Jr., in the center, is flanked by childcare author Dr. Benjamin Spock (left) and (right) by Father Frederick Reed and Cleveland Robinson, president of the Negro American Labor Council.

come perilously close to destroying the fabric of the military and of the nation as a whole. Whether Vietnam had been "winnable" or not was now irrelevant. Homecomings and resettling back into their old lives were often more difficult than facing combat for the first time, and many African Americans in particular made the decision to re-enlist rather than face the poverty and oppression that they had left behind. African

Americans and whites alike often lied about their wounds, claiming that they had suffered an injury in a car crash. Only now, more than forty years since the first U.S. troops were sent to Vietnam, can the veterans openly recall their experiences and the way that the conflict changed their lives and the future of the United States.

In his book *GI Diary,* David Parks recalled, "While serving in Vietnam, I had problems with whites, but the problems didn't compare with the racism I encountered when I returned to America. Perhaps the most positive thing that came out of the war was the comradeship that developed between black and white combat soldiers."

Below: A Vietnam War veteran salutes the flag at a Memorial Day parade in New York in 2002.

COLIN POWELL'S EXPERIENCES OF RACISM

Left: Vietnam veteran and U.S. Secretary of State Colin Powell on his first return visit to Vietnam on July 25, 2001, meets Vietnam's Minister of Foreign Affairs, Nguyen Dy Nien, at the Government Guest House in Hanoi.

Even future Secretary of State Colin Powell was not immune to racism back in 1957 when he attended the Reserve Officers Training Corps (ROTC) summer camp at Fort Bragg, North Carolina. His father, in light of his own exposure to racism and to racial violence in the South, including a lynching in Montgomery, Alabama, warned his son not to leave the camp. Powell worked hard, was awarded "Best Cadet, Company D," and was recognized as the second-best cadet in the camp. His achievements, however, were not celebrated by everyone. A white sergeant explained to Powell: "You think these Southern ROTC instructors are going to go back to their colleges and say the best kid here was a Negro?"

Time Line

1955: October, South Vietnam officially becomes the Republic of Vietnam (RVN).

1962: Military Assistance Command, Vietnam (MACV) is established in Saigon.

1964: August, USS *Maddox* is reportedly attacked by North Vietnamese in Gulf of Tonkin; Congress passes the Gulf of Tonkin Resolution.

1965: October, Private First Class Milton L. Olive III becomes the first African American enlisted man to win the Medal of Honor in Vietnam.

1966: Boxer Muhammad Ali claims status as a conscientious objector on religious grounds.

1967: October, Captain Riley Leroy Pitts becomes the first African American officer to win the Medal of Honor in Vietnam.

1968: January, Tet Offensive is launched; November, future U.S. Secretary of State Colin Powell survives a helicopter crash in Vietnam.

1969: July, one marine is killed and several are injured in racially motivated violence at Marine Corps Base Camp Lejeune, North Carolina; November, 250,000 march in antiwar demonstration in Washington, D.C.

1970: Widespread demonstrations protest the war; December, Congress repeals the Gulf of Tonkin Resolution.

1973: January, peace accords are signed in Paris, France; March, last U.S. ground troops leave Vietnam.

1975: January, North Vietnam announces an all-out offensive to seize South Vietnam; April, last U.S. citizens are evacuated from Saigon; North Vietnamese take Saigon the next day.

Glossary

boycott: refusal to have dealings with a person, store, or organization, usually to express disapproval or to force acceptance of certain conditions

camaraderie: a spirit of mutual trust and friendship

conscientious objector: a person who refuses to fight in the armed forces or bear arms on moral or religious grounds

discrimination: the act of making a difference in treatment or favor on a basis other than individual merit

flak jacket: jacket of heavy fabric reinforced with protective materials designed to stop bullets and shell splinters

induct: to admit someone to a post or organization

infantry: soldiers trained, armed, and equipped to fight on foot

internment: the confinement of a section of society, especially during a war

marginalize: to make or treat as insignificant

segregation: the separation or isolation of a race, class, or ethnic group by enforced or voluntary residence in a restricted area, or by social, educational, or other means

solidarity: unity or agreement of feeling or action, among individuals with a common interest

stereotype: a standardized mental picture that represents an oversimplified opinion, prejudiced attitude, or uncritical judgment

truce: a suspension of fighting by agreement of opposing forces

Further Reading

BOOKS

Emanuel, Edward F. *Soul Patrol.* New York: Ballantine Books, 2003.

Graham, Herman. *Brothers' Vietnam War: Black Power, Manhood, and the Military Experience.* Gainesville, FL: University Press of Florida, 2003.

Terry, Wallace. *Bloods: An Oral History of the Vietnam War by Black Veterans.* New York: Random House, 1984.

Westheider, James E. *Fighting on Two Fronts: African Americans and the Vietnam War.* New York: New York University Press, 1999.

WEB SITES

African Americans in the Vietnam War

www.english.uiuc.edu/maps/poets/s_z/stevens/africanamer.htm
A brief overview of African American service in Vietnam.

African American Involvement in the Vietnam War

www.aavw.org/
This site provides extensive information and links, providing a thorough history of African Americans in Vietnam.

African Americans and the U.S. Navy, Vietnam

www.history.navy.mil/photos/prs-tpic/af-amer/afa-vn.htm
An archive of photos of African American personnel in action in Vietnam.

The Vietnam Conflict: African Americans

www.deanza.edu/faculty/swensson/african_americans.html
This site provides transcripts of broadcast presentations on African Americans and Vietnam.

Index

DUE DATE
